LETTERS TO ROLLINS

R.K. Overton

©1995 2.13.61 Publications

ISBN #1-880985-20-9

DESIGN: Endless   (it figures)

2.13.61

P.O. BOX 1910 · LOS ANGELES ·
CALIFORNIA · 90078 · USA

FOREWORD

I met Henry Rollins in August '88 when I gave him a ride across town to a mutual friend's apartment. In my car, Henry told me he had just found a rare edition of a Henry Miller book in NYC, so I told him my theory about <u>Tropic of Cancer</u> (how Miller had initially intended to call the book <u>International Dateline</u>, but foreseeing early on that the book required a sequel [<u>Tropic of Capricorn</u>], he decided on latitudinal coordinates for both book titles, thus forgoing the temporal confusion often brought on by longitudinal cartographic measurement). Rollins understood completely. He even mentioned once missing his birthday twice because of the International Dateline on an Australian tour.

I knew then that there was more than meets the eye to Henry Rollins, but I also knew it was a waste of time to try and figure him out. I knew that one day I would have my answers, and I let it go at that. Then, one day about a year ago, I was at home flipping through the channels when I came across a re-run of CHiPS. Erik Estrada pulls over a suspicious vehicle and behind the wheel is H.R. Pufnstuf, who's late and on his way to film the Saturday morning television series. The cops decide to let him go, but not before making him divulge the truth about the initials "H.R." At that point, H.R. Pufnstuf looks directly into the camera and says, "Henry Rollins."

It was the information I had been waiting for, the key that unlocked a mystery that had puzzled me for years. You see, Henry Rollins may have a threatening exterior, but children and animals really love him. Dogs, cats... you name it. They're drawn to him like magnets. I was with Henry one time at a petting zoo just north of San Diego, and the deer would not leave him alone. The petting zoo-keeper had to *give* one of those deer to Henry just so that we could leave. Henry kept that deer for a month, nursing him back to health while the little fella's hair grew back in from all that petting, eventually letting him go in the Hollywood hills.

We talked about the vast untapped market out there. "Animals?" Henry asked me.

"No — Children," I told him. I explained how I wanted to present a side of Henry to the world that most people don't know about, the Henry Rollins that I know, the Henry Rollins who arrives at every show of his with a box full of puppies — cute, lovable puppies that he gives out for free. Although I had piqued his interest, Henry put it off for a while – but not before assigning me to a certain task. He put me in charge of his mail for a year. Why he did this, I have no idea, because he knew I had an agenda and that the letters that would catch my eye would tell a different story about Henry Rollins — a story that was potentially damaging to his image and could ruin his career.

1993 was a crossover year for Henry, a weird and wild year of new directions. The letters chosen for this book best chronicle these new directions and their impact on Henry and his audience.

R. K. Overton
August 1994

2/13/93
Dear Henry,

I live on a farm just outside of Iowa City and the local college radio station plays your records a lot. I have pictures of you and your tattoos all over my walls.

You know that Black Flag tattoo on the back of your neck with the four rectangles? Does each of those boxes stand for a different member of the band, and if this is so, which one stands for you? My friend Gary said that you didn't get along with Greg Ginn, so I would assume that there is at least one box between you two acting as a buffer. This is the order that I think is right:

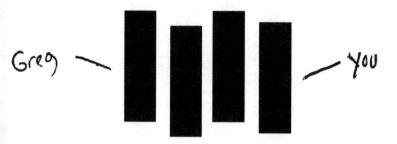

Greg — ▮▮▮▮ — you

By process of elimination, I put you on the right because Greg belongs on the left, since he was left when you moved on.

Now that you're in the Rollins Band, do the boxes in the tattoo stand for the new band members? If so, could you tell me which one is your drummer, Sim Cain?

Also, I have a bet with this guy named George who says the "Search and Destroy" tattoo on your back was changed recently to "Research and Destroy" as a response to new strict rules regarding the use of Exacto-knives in public libraries. If he's wrong, he wants me to tell you to change the tattoo, because the bet was for $100.

Thanks Henry,

Jeff Peterson

Jeff Peterson
Iowa City, IA

RESEARCH & DESTROY

LOCKHART & ASSOCIATES

NEW YORK · LOS ANGELES · BARSTOW

2/13/93

Henry,

As your new publicist, I hope we are off to a great relationship — I know that Jerry didn't work out that well. I just want you to know that I have both the Sesame Street incident and the altercation at Puppet Town under control, press-wise. I know how to handle these people.

I will keep you up to date on everything here in the office. You have my fax numbers, and I have your tour itinerary for Europe and the States.

Sincerely,

Larry Lockhart
Lockhart and Associates

2/13/93

Dear Henry,

Was your last call for "D-4" because that's what the
kid is calling on the cover of the game's box? Well it
was a lucky guess, and it's a hit.

2 in a row. Not bad, Henry.

My next move: F-7

SBP

Steve "Battleship" Potempkin
Austin, Texas

Carol Caldecott
25450 Warner Ave.
Irvine, CA 92745 USA

From the desk of... *Carol Caldecott*

2/13/93

Dear Mr. Rollins,

My 7-year old son Billy loves skateboarding, the Red Hot Chili Peppers, and the Rollins Band. But lately I've had problems getting him to wear knee pads and a helmet when skateboarding because in a recent interview in <u>Thrasher</u> magazine, you said: "Knee pads are for pussies. Helmets too. They take away from the experience."

How could you say such a thing, Henry Rollins? Have you no responsibility for the safety of your fans? How is my impressionable 7-year old son, not to mention his younger brother Timmy, supposed to discern between what's good and bad?

It can't always be <u>my</u> problem! I've already got my hands full with these kids, and I can't always be watching them.

For God's sake, use some common sense, please!

Sincerely,

Carol Caldecott

Carol Caldecott

Dear Henry,

   Are you colorblind? My friend Jill says you're colorblind, and that's why you wear black.

   I saw you on MTV talking about weightlifting. Do you lift weights every day? If you do, don't you get bored? Do you count reps? If you do, do you ever lose count? What do you think about when you lift weights? Do you think about losing count? Do you think about not losing count? What happens if you do lose count? Do you start over?

   Jill also said that your spoken word collection <u>Boxed Life</u> is called that because you punch people. Is that true? I heard that you punched Oscar on Sesame Street. Was that part of some skit?

   Can you be your own pen pal? Does that count? Are we pen pals even though you don't write back? Can I give you a pet name, even though I don't really know you? Can I call you "Smokey"? I like the sound of Smokey Rollins. You can pick a new name for me too if you want.

Your friend,

Kimberly Evans

Kimberly Evans
Raleigh, N.C.

P.S. Happy Birthday Smokey! (I hope you get this by the 13th)

Dear Henry,
your tattoos are cool I live in california too. Maybe you could come over. your friend

Timmy

Dear Henry:

When you get home after months of being on the road, after grueling, never-ending weeks of people in your face — local radio porno promo people and die-hard fans tugging at your shirt, always wanting more more more of your valuable time and demanding every last second of your already waning attention until you are absolutely at your wits end and about to explode — when you are finally at home, alone, and you can shut the door behind you and rest and forget about that crazy world out there, do you ever take off your clothes and stand with your taut, muscular, naked body in front of the full-length bathroom mirror and tHink to yourself: "I am Jesus!"
A   Awestruck at first by the sheer power behind this thought, you stare at your face in the mirror and this time you say the words out loud, softly at first, with a gentleness and reverence for the man behind them: "I am Jesus." You say the words again, and then again and again, each time a little louder than before. And for a brief second, you become lost in the moment as the words run together like a mantra: "IamJesusIamJesusIamJesusIamJesusIamJesus."
        But you catch yourself, and a smile appears on your face as the words suddenly change in meaning from a simple mantra into a very powerful affirmation: "I am Jesus!" You begin to speak louder and more forcefully, and the words flow from your mouth with an eloquence and ease and XXXXXXX intensity un-matched by even JamEs Earl Jones: "I am Jesus, I am Jesus, I am Jesus!" And with this moving proclamation, you feel something building up inside of you, an assurance, an awe-inspiring level of confidence that is just now awakening. It is as though you have finally arrived and are announcing something wonderful and profound to the world, something you have known all along that other people, stuck in their pre-conceived notions, might not have recognized in you.
        "I am Jesus!" you vehemently declare, clenching your fist for emphasis. YOu say it again, and in the deafening silence that follows, you suddenly feel the inspiraton of Charlton Heston, and you add for even more emphasis: "By God, I am Jesus!" And this new phrase now becomes the affirmation and you repeat it over and over, experimenting with different deliveries, emphasizing certain syllables over others: "By God, I am Jesus. By God, I am Jesus. By God I am Jesus!"
        And then it happens. You begin to feel a warmth all over your body, a kind of tingling that you instantly recognize as a heightened sense of joy. The tears on your face are from laugh-ter as you run naked through the rooms of your home shouting "I am Jesus! I am Jesus, by God, I am Jesus! I AM THE NAZ!" YOu run back into the bathroom and begin to fill the bathtub with water — not too full, but just deep enough that when you step into the tub you are actually walking on water. Youget out of the tub and dry off the bottom s of your feet and go into the kitchen to see what's in the fridge and all there is, is a half gallon of water. You close the refrigerator door and then quickly reopen it to find that, miraculously, the water hAs turned into Wwine. So you call over 12 of your best friends for a little XXXXXX get-together and pretty soon the party gets out of hand and someone calls the cops. When the cops arrive, you

are furious and demand to know who made the complaint. Eerily, the fcops verify that the complaint came from a phone _inside_ your house and must have been made by one of the 12 people you invited to your party. And as you get hauled away and the neighbors cast nasty stone- faced glances, you wonder which of your friendS betrayed you and if any of this was really worth the trouble. But in your heart, you know it was well worth it, for an event of this magnitude only comes along once every 2000 years.

  Henry , I feel your pain.

Lynn Weir

Dear Henry,

I got your form letter about how much fan mail you've been getting, and I really think it sucks that you give priority to prisoners and kids in youth homes. What am I supposed to do, hot-wire a couple of cars and do some local time just to get your attention? What about kids in hospitals? Do you write to them too? If I was a poster child, I bet you'd write.

For now, what if I just include a self-addressed stamped envelope with a blank piece of paper for you to write on? Could you just send me a letter? You at least owe me that, because I have all your books and CD's.

Sincerely,

Rusty Jenkins
Janesville, Wisconsin

Rusty J.

2/13/93

"Fun flies when you're doing time"
— Henry Rollins on the set of <u>The Chase</u>.

"The fourth dimension is a waste of my space and time."
— Henry Rollins interview, <u>Thrasher</u> magazine

"Because there is no space without time, and no time like the present, then we can only assume that the future begins tomorrow."
— Henry Rollins interview, KCRW FM

Dear Henry,

I agree with your friend at Jet Propulsion Labs that the above quotes, when juxtaposed with the artwork from your album <u>LIFE TIME</u>, do shed some new light on your interpretation of the time-space continuum. At first glance, it might not seem so obvious whether you view time as a separate dimension that flows at an even rate, independent of space (classical physics), or if you subscribe to relativity theory, where time and space cannot be separated, and time is added to the three spatial coordinates as a fourth dimension.

As for the art work on the cover of <u>LIFE TIME</u>, there are two possible interpretations. Fatalistically, living life is experienced as *doing time* — life as a prison sentence — feeling at the mercy of a world shaped by someone or some *thing* greater than you. On the other hand, the more positive outlook puts you in the driver's seat, having *the time* of your life. Where life is something to live to the fullest — a free will stance with you shaping your world with your own hands (life in the moment, life in the now).

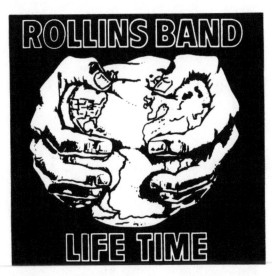

Henry, do you think it's just a coincidence that your motto is "Do It"? And by extension, doesn't this mean Do It Now? But why is it necessary to do it now, Henry? Is it because you think that there's only a certain amount of time left to live, and so why not make the best of it (time as a given--the Classic Euclidean outlook)? Or is it that time is completely relative, so why not make the best of it?

Are we confusing the map with the territory, Henry? Or does the answer lie in your other motto: "part animal/part machine"? For if you really are part animal and part machine, then YOU HENRY ROLLINS ARE A TERMINA-TOR! And that is why you SEARCH AND DESTROY. And since by definition all Terminators are Time Travelers, then you have the ability to operate outside of space and time, and therefore you have a relativistic view of time.

Albert Einstein believed there is only one absolute in a relativistic time frame; that this one "truth" is the only constant in our multidimensional world. Here now is that truth. Remember it always:

Dwarf Time is Short Ended.

Until next time, Henry.

Rob Overton

Dear Henry,

My little niece Polly just loved your appearance on Sesame Street, when you did songs from your children's record <u>NAP TIME</u>. Since I got her <u>NAP TIME</u> a month ago, she's been listening to it day-in and day-out. She especially likes "Kangaroo Tattoo", and the squealing noises on "Pigfucker". She wants to know if those are real rabbit's necks snapping in "Petshop", or just studio effects.

I wanted to congratulate you on outselling Raffi in this new market. It takes a lot of guts to change direction like you did, and I admire that. I think it's good for children to hear songs about life and death, to get them ready for the real world. God knows we're headed in a downward spiral. Sure, Erma Bombeck would say that Life isn't a bowl of cherries, that the grass is always greener over the septic tank, but I say fuck Erma Bombeck, Henry. Nobody thinks she's funny anymore. Lou Reed's painter friend Donald would say "Stick a fork in her ass and turn her over, she's done."

I'm optimistic, though. The glass isn't half empty, it's full, but full of God knows what. It's true, we may be eating shit. Well okay, that's a given. But Henry, in that shit you'll find peanuts, and in the peanuts, protein. But most of us are still saying "Hey! Waiter, there's shit in my soup!" you know? I say own up to it, you ordered it!

Take it easy,

Your pal Lyle Wilcox

Lyle

P.S. Butch "the Oreo King" told me to tell you not to worry about the club owners stiffing bands in Georgia, that the sodomy laws in that state are set up to protect you from that type of behavior.

Henry

You might not remember me, but you punched me once in
10th grade. Right in the face. In Gym. I had it coming.
Anyway, I'm not writing to bring that up, I'm writing
to tell you I was there when you punched our manager
after your performance at Puppet Town. He's really an
asshole, and he definitely had it coming.

I'm the junior assistant manager, and on days of per-
formances I double as balloon-animal wrangler. Some-
times I fill the balloons with nitrous oxide instead of
helium, just to get by (you try filling up balloons in
front of 400 screaming kids).

I haven't had this job for very long. Before this, my
brother-in-law talked me into investing the money my
Grandma left me in an ice cream truck venture. He was
going to drive the truck, but then my sister filed for
divorce and he left town. I had no choice but to take
over driving. On my first day out, I had a meltdown. My
ex-brother-in-law forgot to fix a freon gas leak in the
freezer unit, and before I knew it, I was up to my
ankles in soggy Eskimo Pies. The Mr. Freezes and the
Push-Ups were the last to melt, which is weird, because
they're usually the softest.

I guess I went kinda nuts. I turned up the volume and
blasted that stupid theme from "Love Story" out those
shitty speakers, scaring the neighbor kids and killing
a dogg as I drove 50 miles per hour down the side-
walks. I eventually hit a UPS truck. My license got
revoked for a year, but no one pressed charges. They
were okay to hire me here at PUppet Town, even if
they're idiots.

CARL PLASKE
Trenton, NJ

3/5/93

Dear Henry,

You lucky stiff! D-5 was a hit too, but I'm still standing.

And by the way, nice try on your proposition of speeding things up with 2 moves per correspondence. If things were neck and neck, I would lose because you started first. No way Henry, I'm not stupid.

It sounds as though you've figured out just how long this game could last. At the most, with a 10 x 10 board we will finish the game in 100 moves, which, at one move per week clocks in at a game of Battleship lasting 4 years long (100 moves *per person* doubles the time involved). At the least, the game can be finished in 17 moves per person (5 holes in the Aircraft Carrier, 4 in the Battleship, 3 in the Cruiser, 3 in the Submarine, and 2 in the Destroyer), a 34 week period or almost 9 months.

By accepting my challenge to play Battleship through the U.S. Mail, you have signed on until the end, through sickness and through health, until death do us part. Let's face it, Henry, it's not exactly like we're playing chess, or Stratego, games that require a certain amount of thought. It's really just a slow process of elimination, and in our case, one that involves a great deal of trust — trust that neither of us is moving our ships.

And yes, I might consider playing by mail until you're in Austin again, and we can finish the game in person.

Next move: E-1

SBP

Steve "Battleship" Potempkin
Austin, Texas

3/15/93
Dear Henry,

If you were a cop, would the tattoo on your back read "Search and Seizure"? This guy at school who's really into you says you give yourself pre-concert enemas. His name is Jay and he claims that you're hooked on colonics. He also says you have a tattoo of your face on your ass. True?

Have you ever been hypnotized? My brother Kirby and I hypnotized a frog last week, rubbing his head with a stick. We weren't sure how to unhypnotize him, so Kirby tweaked him on the head with his thumb. Then we tried to hypnotize my Grandma, because we wanted to find if she likes my mom more than our aunt. My Grandma, when she stays with us calls my mom by my aunt's name, and when she's at my aunt's house she calls her by my mom's name (about 5 years ago Grandma had a stroke, so she's not as tuned in as she used to be). Anyway, we found out through hypnosis that Grandma likes my mom better. But since she's had a stroke, her answers may not be all that accurate, right? We might have been "leading the witness".

Are you related to Sonny Rollins? I see his name all the time in record stores. I know for sure that you're not related to Howard Rollins, the guy on <u>In the Heat of the Night</u>. And what about Rollins Trucking Company? Do you ever haul your equipment in a ROLLINS truck? They could be your corporate sponsor.

Jay wants to know if you ever shave your head anymore.
The neighbor kids had to shave their heads last summer because
of ringworm. Everyone said they got it from kissing dogs. Is
this possible? If you had your own summer camp, Camp Rollins,
would you make the kids shave their heads? I bet you would.

See ya,

Jeff Peterson
Iowa City, IA

P.S. Henry, did you know you're protecting my neighbor's
house?

3/19/93

Dear Henry,

I looked into your question about thermostat timers, and from what you said about the weird clicking noise that the timer dial makes before your thermostat shuts off, it sounds like your time reference indicator should be re-set.

Keeping in mind that the third electrician in any operation is always referred to as "the ground", this is what you should do:

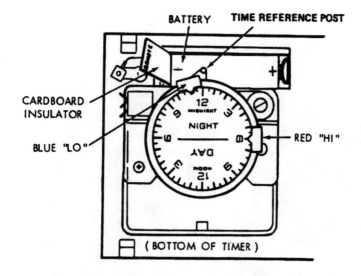

1) Grab the largest regular screwdriver that you can find. (The longer the better as it is needed for leverage).

2) Holding the screwdriver pointed toward you, lift the top portion of the snap-on indicator away from the timing mechanism, leaving a space between the dial face and the time reference post.

3) After the snap-on indicator clears the upper ridge, shift the time reference post down toward the timing mechanism at the bottom of the dial.

If the screwdriver should slip due to excessive force, clean and bandage your wound, taking time to remove any blood from the wall or general thermostat area.

4) Pulling the timer dial away from the toggle matrix, snip the white wire leading to the back of the polarity terminal and snap on the thermostat cover.

And there you have it, Henry, in 4 easy steps.

Bad news about the latest '70's trends coming back to haunt us in the '90's: Some idiot in Michigan is trying to get the metric system back on line in the U.S., claiming that in 5 years, the English system of measurement will be virtually obsolete.

So beware! And if all else fails, Think Metric.

Rob Overton

3/29/93
Dear Henry,

You can gloat all you want because you sank my
Battleship, but I've got 4 ships left, and I haven't
lost this game in 5 years. Call it intuition or just
good offensive strategy, but you're dealing with the
best. I know who you are Henry Rollins, and I know
where you're hiding.

My call: G-2

SBP
Steve "Battleship" Potempkin
Austin, Texas

Dear Smokey,

I read an article about how you punched that guy in Australia who ran at you onstage, and then wound up with his teeth in your hand. That must have hurt. Do you have any pictures of you punching that guy? Are there pictures of you punching anyone? Have you ever been punched on stage? Even accidentally?

My cousin Fred once tried to stage dive at a show of yours in Chicago, and as he was getting up on stage, you punched him right in the face and gave him a bloody nose. Do you remember that? Do you punch someone at every show? Are that guy's teeth still in your hand? Did you have to get rabies shots?

About a year ago in the paper, there was an article about this man in Seattle who had a tooth growing out of the bottom of his foot — right in the arch area. I don't know if it was a molar or an incisor or what, but I do remember that he wasn't sure whether he should go to a dentist or a podiatrist. He ended up wearing special orthodontic shoes.

I wanted to ask you something, Smokey. There was a Guns-N-Roses special on MTV, and I got in a fight with Jill's neighbor Luci who was over, because she said that sometimes you wore chaps onstage. I said no way would Henry Rollins wear chaps onstage! Come on! You wouldn't wear pants with no ass, would you Smokey?

Also, I've asked around at record stores about your favorite record, Iggy Pop's Farmhouse, but no one seems to think it's still in print.

Your friend,

Kimberly Evans

Kimberly Evans
Raleigh, N.C.

P.S. Be Careful!

Dear Henry,

Of all the dumb luck. Since I last wrote and yelled at you for only responding to convicts and teens in youth homes, I myself have been sent to our local Juvenile Detention Center. I really have, I swear. You'll notice I did not include my return address here at the Detention Center. That's because we're not allowed mail or visitors who are non-family members. So you can write me "care of" my mom (her name is Betsy) at my house and she will make sure I get your letter.

I really feel I've learned my lesson, Henry. Crime doesn't pay. If you can't do the time, don't do the crime. Friends don't let friends drive drunk. Better safe than never.

Sincerely,

Rusty Jenkins
Janesville, Wisconsin

Rusty J.

P.S. The food here is really bad (worse than the cafeteria at school). So hurry up and send your letter.

Carol Caldecott
25450 Warner Ave.
Irvine, CA 92745 USA

From the desk of... *Carol Caldecott*

4/1/93

Dear Mr. Rollins,

I just received your letter, and frankly, I am very angry with you. Do you only respond to people you want to insult? Am I supposed to think it's funny, you telling me to wear my son's kneepads? What exactly are you implying? That type of innuendo is absolutely uncalled for.

I've done some research on you, my son has articles, and it doesn't surprise me a bit that you were in one of the most violent punk rock bands of the eighties. And this "Search and Destroy", what kind of motto is that? What kind of role model are you? Your music starts fights in the audience, and I happen to know that the PMRC is not happy with you or the lyrics to your songs.

Shape up, Henry Rollins.

Sincerely,

Carol Caldecott

Carol Caldecott

Dear Henry,
How come you don't
wriet songs about
boogers or spiders?

your friend timmy

timmy

4/11/93
Henry —

I know you're down to the wire proofreading your Black Flag
book, but I don't want you to lose sight of this fact: The days
of Black Flag were crazy times, and the punctuation in the
book should reflect this. I don't just want people to read the
book and think, "Jesus, they did a gig in Denver and only one
guy showed up." I want them to think, "Christ, that Rollins
sure has a weird theory on semicolons." I want them to read
the book with a red pen, and send it back with comments like
"Avoid gratuitous modifiers." I want it to make each reader
think so hard, he'll have question marks coming out his ass.

Remember: When in doubt, use exclamation marks. Drive it
home with a fucking hammer.

Butch the Oreo King

4/15/93

Dear Henry,

Before you joined Black Flag, when you worked in that pet shop in Washington D.C., did you ever pretend that you were working in a tiny zoo where they sold the animals? And people would come in asking to see the tigers, and you'd have to say "No tigers today, sir. But we do have some wonderful field mice."

Or when you worked at Haagen-Dazs, did you ever think that with each scoop you were somehow one step closer to saving the world?

Sometimes I think I'd like to work at Disneyland, maybe as the guy inside the Mickey Mouse costume. Then I could be invisible, and no one would know it was me. I figure I'd have to start as one of the other characters, like one of the Seven Dwarfs, and eventually work my way up to Mickey. There's probably some sort of Disney character hierarchy. Like first you start as a Dwarf (probably Dopey), then you work your way up to Doc, then you're no longer a Dwarf and they let you be Pluto, then Goofy, then Mickey.

Or maybe it has less to do with characters and more to do with locations. Maybe you have pay your dues working on one of the shitty rides, like the spinning teacups, and gradually work your way up to Space Mountain. Or maybe everyone starts in Frontierland and works their way towards Fantasyland.

I really don't care about getting a job, not now. It's all my parents talk about, like I'm supposed to know now what I want to do. I just think that one day I'll know what to do, and until then, I guess I wait it out. Did you know what you wanted to do when you were 16?

I have to go.

Jeff Peterson

Jeff Peterson
Iowa City, IA

P.S. Are you ever going to do a whole CD of Christmas songs?

4/25/93

Dear Henry,

I'm curious, have you run out of ideas and now you're
just copying my moves? Did "G-2" just happen to pop in
your head after reading my last letter, or have you
asked one of your flunkies to keep up this game with me
while you're off in Europe or Australia or wherever it
is that they think you're God?

G-2 was a hit, you prick, and don't get all excited
because you've had 5 hits in a row. The odds are in-
creasingly against you, Henry. Anyone will tell you
that there is an ebb and a flow to Battleship. There
are peaks and valleys, just like in real life, so get
ready to play a shitty hand.

And quit copying my moves.

My next call: I-6

SBP

Steve Potempkin
Austin, Texas

LOCKHART & ASSOCIATES

NEW YORK · LOS ANGELES · BARSTOW

4/26/93

Henry,

As you know, the <u>NAP TIME</u> video has been in the Top 5 of the Billboard Children's Chart for over 10 weeks now and just this week surpassed Disney's re-release of <u>The Rescuers Down Under</u>. Of course, the exposure this has brought you has been wonderful, with record and video sales skyrocketing and the demand for personal appearances just slightly under that for the cast of NBC's <u>Blossom</u>. However, as your publicist, I must inform you that there has been a great deal of pressure from your newfound children's audience to clean up your image.

The kids aren't the problem here, Henry. They think you're the best. It's the parents who are raising a stink, and from the mail and phone calls we've received, the problem seems to be your tattoos. I think it's a generational thing. To people who grew up in the 50's and 60's, tattoos are equated with drunken sailors and nasty biker brawls. But kids these days don't have those preconceptions. In fact, from an informal survey we conducted with children between the ages of 2 and 4 at your most recent Puppet Town appearance, we found that kids are really quite intrigued by your tattoos. More than a few were heard to say that the reason they liked your videotapes over Barney's was that "Barney doesn't have a snake on his leg."

So we have a couple of options, Henry. First we could appease the parents, using tattoos to your advantage. A tattoo that reads "BIKE SAFETY" or "UNICEF" strategically placed on one of your upper arms could do wonders.

The second option, which I tend to like better, is that we distract them. Fuck appeasement. Who wants to cater to the whims of self-righteous parents? I'd much rather cater to the whims of a 4-year old.

So here's the plan. Every celebrity has their cause. Jerry has his kids, Sally Struthers has hers, and although we could make an easy argument that Jerry's kids are better fed than Sally's, this is precisely the point I want to make. Sally Struthers has bitten off more than she can chew. Her eyes are bigger than their stomachs. Solve world hunger and help third world kids find foster parents? GOOD LUCK! We're all too familiar with celebrity causes, the list goes on and on, and curing all these problems seems so futile.

So when it comes to your celebrity cause, we approach it differently. I've done some research and discussed children's diseases with some specialists. There's a bone disorder called Perthes Disease that strikes young children down in their prime, between the ages of 4 and 9. With this particular bone disorder, which tends to afflict boys more often than girls, the ball and socket joint of the hip deteriorates, leaving the child immobile.

Imagine: a 5-year old child, helpless and unable to walk, is forced to watch his playmates from the sidelines. This bone deterioration can have a devastating effect on the young child's psyche.

But here's the catch: after the ball in the socket of the hip joint deteriorates, IT GROWS BACK. It grows back, Henry! Miraculous! It's a disease with a built-in 100% success rate, a guaranteed cure. Like a second row of teeth. Or puberty. And the kids, as it turns out, CAN WALK, with the help of special leg braces or crutches.

You can't go wrong, Henry. It's a children's disease that sounds worse than it really is. It doesn't strike that many children — maybe 1500 a year, and depending on the age, it heals in 7 months to a year and a half. But we don't even have to tell people that it heals itself. They'll see those kids with crutches, kids who with the help of just a few dollars from each viewer will be able to have a leg brace to make things easier. The money wouldn't go toward a cure, because there already is a cure — time. The money would buy orthopedic supplies and pay medical costs for families without any money.

So basically, we'll have distracted these parents who are harassing you by focusing on helping afflicted children, ultimately boosting your image in the eyes of both the parents and the kids who are your prime demographic target in this market anyway.

Let me know what you think, Henry.

Sincerely,

Larry Lockhart
Lockhart and Associates

Dear Smokey,

I hope you come to Raleigh soon. I don't even care if you're just doing spoken word without your band. My best friend Jill says it's your upper body tattoos that she likes, but for me it's those cute black shorts that I love. I mean, your tattoos are cool, but there's something about those shorts, Smokey.

Where did you get those shorts? In New York City? I would really like a pair. Is there any way you could send me a pair of your shorts? I would pay you. My friend Jill says that because you only wear black you probably have a whole bunch of pairs. I say you have two pairs. Am I right? Do you wear underwear?

I know that's a personal question. You don't have to answer it. I'll answer anything you want to know about me.

I want to get a tattoo, but my mom and dad won't let me. They say I have to wait until I'm 18, but that's stupid. I don't want to wait 5 years.

Can I get a newsletter?

Thanks alot Smokey.

With love,

Kimberly Evans

Kimberly Evans
Raleigh, N.C.

5/3/93

Dear Henry,

Regarding our conversation the other night about "tea-weights," I checked with the potpourri shop down the street, and they said that it's not a "tea-weight", but a "T-weight". Although they can still be used to hold down floating tea bags, it's their shape that gives them the name. Normally they're found on Nautilus machines.

As for that guy at the spoken word show in Philly who wanted you to read from <u>The Hobbit</u>, those Tolkien freaks are an odd bunch, and if you give in to their every want and need, they'll eat you alive. They're not used to anyone paying them any attention outside of Star Trek conventions.

Also, I spoke to a geneticist out at Cal Tech about the title to your book <u>Pissing in the Gene Pool</u>, and she verified that 1 in 10 people have a certain coding in their RNA that turns red on contact with urine. It is usually located in the messenger RNA and curiously, it is a widespread genetic trait among Olympic swimmers. Crick and Watson discovered something similar in their DNA experiments with chlorine. So who's to say the swim coach is the only person who can pinpoint the bladder problems of the swimmer in lane 3?

Finally, the kid in Iowa with the questions about ringworm might be relieved to know that the recent surge in my own neighborhood's ringworm-related head shavings has been traced to a Sheltie-mix named Kipper who still sports an impressive array of follicular mange on his eyebrows and lower Carol Lombard regions.

Keep the questions coming, Henry!

Rob Overton

Henry

I've been reading your books lately. They're okay read-
ing, but too repetitious. I just got done with
Deathgrip and 1000 Ways to Die, and I can think of
about 50 other ways to Kkill people. It's really been
on my mind since I got fired from PUppet Town. My boss,
the guy you punched, found out I put a personal ad
under his name in American Ventriloquist magazine. His
wife was getting all these phone calls at the house and
thought he was two-timing her. So he fired me. In a
way, it's your fault that I got fired, because I never
would have had the guts to put the ad in the magazine
if you hadn't punched him XXXXX first.

I've been reading about serial killers, and the one guy
who really impresses me is the one guy they never
caught: the Zodiac Killer. He was in the Bay Area in
the 70's and early 80'z, then just disappeared. You
correspond with Charlie Manson, so you know what goes
on in the mind of someone like the Zodiac Killer. So do
I. I think that between murders, he's thinking: "Hey, I
haven't killed an y Gemini's in a while." And so the
key question becomes how to find out someone's birthday
without them knowing or suspecting. L ike I know your
birthday, but you don't know mine.

This guy probably dOesn't have any friends. I doubt he
hangs out at Denny's, hoping to hear if someone gets a
free birthday meal. He probably has access to informa-
tion terminals or is in a position to see driver's
licenses. Maybee he's got the perfect angle for a
serial Killer. With a pick-up linelike "What's your
sign ?" he may get turned down, but most people will
give up the inforMmation.

Do you think he's schizzo, HEnry? Do you think I'm
schizzo to be reading about him? I'm just doing re-
search, in a way, and I don't care what you think.
X
See you soon,

CARL PLASKE

5/18/93

Dear Henry,

As you know, I receive stacks of mail every week from all walks of golfkind. From frustrated, junior varsity, fourth-string rookies to star-struck, geriatric level two three-holers. Now I can't answer all of my mail, and I have been known on occasion to stoke the fireplace in my living room if the mail gets to be a bit much, but I do get to see most of the letters that are fortunate enough to be at the top of the heap. Plus, the sponsors of my weekly program, Slice soda, have been on my case to answer the more typical golf questions to reach a broader audience.

Your question — what to do when your ball gets buried in the sand near the lip of the trap — is a very common problem. The trouble here is that there's not much green to work with, and you can feel like you're in quite a jam.

Most people have problems with this shot because they think the solution lies in their swing. It doesn't. Technically, this situation is known as a "Buried Lie, Up Close," and although it may very well be an outward manifestation of the problems you are having with your parents, here is a simple recovery shot. Before you reach for that Texas Wedge, think again. Instead, get out your putter, or better yet, bring along *your dad's putter.* Keeping the clubface at a 90 degree angle to the incline of the sand trap lip, pick the club straight up, cocking your wrists as little as possible. In a frenzied, sweeping motion, pull the clubhead straight down to a spot 4 inches to the right of the ball (assuming you are right handed). Do not follow through. The distance the ball travels will be inversely proportional to the angle of the clubface at impact. Next, simply bend the putter back to its original shape, and feign indifference as the others stand in awe of your golfing expertise.

NOTE: Before attempting this shot, make sure that the lip of the sand trap does not overhang so much as to make the shot impossible. If there is a dangerous overhang, stamp it down with the heel of your foot so that the ball will clear the lip. This is commonly known as "lip therapy", although there is still some question about its legality among golf experts.

If for some fluke in nature the ball is still under the lip (and the sand cloud has not yet settled), swiftly kick the ball out of the trap with the toe of your right foot. To create a diversion, point to where you think you saw the ball land, and when the other golfers look in that direction, this is your cue to kick. "Clubfooting" or "the Kickback" as it's known in Scotland, is generally more acceptable today in European golf circles than on PGA fairways, where it is about as welcome as drunken hecklers or skeet shooters.

Keep in the swing of things!

Your golf guru,
Chip Taylor

5/23/93

Jesus, Rollins, are you happy? You just sank another of
my boats. But I must point out that it was the Cruiser
you sank this time, the most lightweight boat of the
whole Battleship game. Ask anyone in the Navy, and
they'll laugh in your face and tell you the real truth:
CRUISERS ARE FOR PUSSIES.

It's a fucking patrol boat and not even heavily armed,
at that. So I hope you're proud of yourself, you just
sank the Chess equivalent of a pawn. The Gulf War
equivalent of bombing the shit out of an Iraqi baby
milk factory.

And how would you have done it if this were a real-life
game of Battleship out on the ocean, huh Henry? Would
you have used your submarine, hiding under water like a
coward? Ooooooooohhhhhh, I'm shakin' in my boats!

I may only have 3 ships left, but it is you who will
either sink or swim in this game, Rollins. I guarantee
it.

Next move: A-7 (I'm so sure of myself, Henry, that I'm
already putting a red pin on the board for what will be
my first in a string of hits)

Yours truly,

SBP

Steve "Battleship" Potempkin
Austin, Texas

Dear Henry,

   I still haven't gotten a letter from you, and it is really important that I get something in the mail from you as soon as possible, because another complication has come up. I know you're really busy, but I thought you'd want to know that I have taken ill and am in the infirmary here at the Detention Center in my hometown. I really am. I know how the first letter I sent may have given you the impression that I would do anything to be on your priority list for answering letters — even lie about being in a youth home — but that isn't the case now, I swear. So here I am in the hospital. I overheard some doctors in the hall yesterday, and they said something about there only being six months left, if it doesn't spread too quickly to the upper clavicle region. So it sounds pretty serious. We're hoping it doesn't develop into muscular dystrophy or cancer, or tuberculosis. That would suck.
   So you have to write to me now, because I'm racing against the clock. You don't want to have that kind of guilt on your conscience, do you? Remember to send the letter c/o my mom (Betsy), and send it to my house, not the Detention Center Hospital, because the doctors don't want me receiving any mail at the hospital because it might interfere with my healing process. They don't understand that a letter from you would really cheer me up and maybe even give me a reason to live.

Sincerely,

Rusty Jenkins
Janesville, Wisconsin

Rusty J.

P.S. The food here at the hospital really stinks and everyone is mean to me.

KROK RADIO
109.5 FM
"Mostly Music, Just Right of the Dial"

5/24/93

2.13.61 people:

I first want to say how excited we all are here at **KROK** that The ROLLINS BAND will be appearing at our **KROK** Barbeque Bash in June. From the early planning stages on, The ROLLINS BAND has been our number one choice of alternative bands to headline the Bash. However, it is with utmost regret that I must relay a slight change in plan regarding the event itself.

Due to unforeseen budget constraints, most notably the creative accounting of **KROK**'s ex-financial supervisor, **KROK** will be unable to provide the food and beverages as originally promised in our radio ad campaigns. Therefore, as it is put forth in paragraph 3, lines 12-14 of our event agreement, the onus now falls on the recording artists/bands themselves to provide the food supplies for their fans.

To make this easier on the bands involved, we here at **KROK** have taken the liberty of drawing the names of specific picnic items from a large revolving fishbowl, randomly assigning each of these items to a different recording artist/band. Because there are over 20 picnic items and less than 7 bands playing at the Bash, the average band will be responsible for at least three picnic items.

The following items must be supplied by The ROLLINS BAND :

1) HOT DOG BUNS (at least 15,000)
2) MUSTARD
3) UMBRELLAS
4) SECURITY

Thank you for your understanding, and again, we look forward to seeing The ROLLINS BAND perform at **KROK**'s Barbeque Bash on June 6.

Sincerely,

Bob Devries
Publicity/Promotion Chairman
KROK FM

cc: 2.13.61 Publications
    Rollins Management

Dear Henry,

Butch "the Oreo King" is trying to unload this '79 Lincoln Continental because he can't get the smell of urine out of the trunk. I figured a tailgate party at the Meadowlands got a little out of hand, but he said something about ransom money and how there was a mix-up with the drop site but how he thought there'd still be enough money for a new car. Maybe he'd better find a new line of work. Any suggestions? He wants to know if you're in the market for a new truck to haul your band's equipment. He said he could get you one for next to nothing. I'm sure he could. A real steal.

By the way, Butch got his nickname at age 5, when he was the only neighborhood kid able to put four whole Oreo cookies in his mouth at the same time. Needless to say, we were all quite impressed. I'd hate to think how many he can fit in his mouth now.

Later, Henry,

Lyle Wilcox *Lyle*

P.S. How long should you wait to do pull-ups after a shoulder separation? My friend Dave says a week, and my wife Penelope says I should switch to a gravity guidance system. Also, my little niece Polly wants to know if you sold your hoppity-hops, she really liked the blue one.

Dear Henry,

You watch Star Trek, right? I mean The Next Generation (TNG), not Deep Shit Nine (where they don t go anywhere). I got in a big fight with my brother about how Geordi LaForge s visor works. He says that the visor scans the electromagnetic spectrum up to 50,000 TerraHtz, converts the data into usable frequencies, and then transmits that information directly to Geordi s brain. I tell him that he s wrong, that the range of the visor goes up to 100,000 TerraHtz, and that the visor doesn t just convert the data, it *compresses* it. So then he starts whining like he always does, saying that ▌if the electromagnetic spectral range of the visor is as high as you say it is, then wouldn t the stress levels at that conversion rate be too much for Geordi s cerebral cortex to handle?▌ So I give it all back to him in a manner that his 8th grade, B-minus in Science mind can handle. First of all, I say, ▌the data from the visor goes into Geordi s *visual* cortex, not his cerebral cortex. And secondly, it s not a steady stream of data that enters his brain. A bank of preprocessors compresses the data stream into *pulses* so as to avoid a sensory overload.▌ And then my brother says, in that one-upmanship smug-fuck tone that he has, ▌A bank of preprocessors? A Bank?▌

So I say, ▌Not a *Bank*-bank, asshole, where you put your money. It s a data bank that is small enough to fit in his visor. This is the 24th Century! Believe me, they have the technology.▌

So being the dork that he is, my brother runs and gets the TNG Technical Manual and turns to where it talks about Geordi s VISOR (an acronym for Visual Instrument and Sensory Organ Replacement). He points out that it says nothing about a bank of preprocessors converting the data stream into pulses. So I break it to him nicely, about how in the 5th season, in The Masterpiece Society (episode 213), Geordi explains how his visor works to Hannah Bates, the chief scientist from the Moab IV colony, a colony whose Biosphere is threatened by a core fragment on a collision course with the planet. Geordi tells Hannah that the high energy pulse compression routine going through his visor has to be short enough to avoid overloading his emitter arrays.

So that shut my brother up. Can you believe I have to put up with that kind of shit? Was your brother a jerk like mine growing up? Was he as stupid about lower lateral sensor arrays and warp core breach as my brother? Didn t you just want Lt. Worf to kick his ass?

You re in Hollywood, Henry. Is this really TNG s last season?

Sincerely,

Edward Dyson
Providence, RI

6/4/93

Dear Smokey,

I just watched my tape of you on Dennis Miller from last year, and those cute black shorts of yours were riding pretty low, so my guess is that you weren't wearing underwear. Am I right? I've heard that some performers don't wear underwear onstage, but they do wear it offstage, like Chris Robinson of the Black Crowes. Jill told me that his pants were so tight one time on stage that he passed out. Has that ever happened to you? If it did happen to you, would you just say you collapsed from exhaustion?

How come at your spoken word shows you wear a shirt, but you don't when you're with the Rollins Band? I liked that Gap ad you did. I saw it in <u>Rolling Stone</u> and put it on the wall next to my bed. Do you shop at the Gap? Did they give you free clothes? I would love it if someone gave me free clothes. Did they only give you black clothes? Do you think the Baby Gap is dumb? My sister says that babies don't care what they wear. My niece is 15 months old and she hates clothes, she'd rather run around naked.

Do you wear make-up onstage? What about offstage? Jill says you do. She just got a tattoo and her parents are really pissed. She's a year older than me, and her parents are even weirder than mine.

I just got your newsletter, and I'm really excited about your show here this summer. The only other time I saw you was on the Lollapalooza tour. At that time I was really into Jane's Addiction. Jill had 9th row seats, and if we hadn't been that close I might never have noticed your cute black shorts!

I've enclosed a photo of my cat Virgil. It's only half a picture because my dad was in the upper corner and I cut him out.

Do you think I could meet you when you are here? I hope so.

See you soon.

Your friend,

Kimberly Evan

Kimberly Evans
Raleigh, N.C.

6/17/93

Boy that response was quick! What, do you have a little
extra time on your hands these days, Henry? All the
press about that ugly skirmish on Sesame Street got you
down? Gee, that's something for your resume, punching
one of the Muppets. But isn't that a felony?
Puppeteering? So who's pulling the strings now, Henry?
Will you be made an example of by the new Puppetmaster
General?

It's really quite appropriate for us to be talking
about puppets, Henry, because it seems to me that I
specifically asked you to stop copying my Battleship
moves. And now you send your next move as A-7? That was
my last move, or was there some sort of mix-up in the
mail. If you're going to mimic my moves, why not just
stamp the last letter you received with "Return to
Sender." It won't cost you anything. You just hold my
letter up to the light, see what coordinates I've
called for my next move, and then pop it in the mailbox
on back to me.

You're so predictable, Rollins. Just think how wonder-
ful your life would be if you actually had access to
original thought. Oh I forget, you already do have
access to original thoughts - my original thoughts!

Incidentally, your call for A-7 is a hit. Lucky guess.

My next move: D-1

Later,

SBP

Steve Potempkin
Austin, Texas

6/21/93
Dear Henry,

I really liked the Haiku you read the other night at the Christian Science Remedial Reading Room in Westwood, but found myself overwhelmed by the mathematics of it all. I was especially confused by the poem that went:

> Iambic Pentameter
> Rings more true to me
> Than any form of Haiku.

Then I realized it was Reverse Haiku (7-5-7), not Russian Metric with a 7-5-10 signature like you said. It was the first time in a while that I had felt a numbers crunch, and I remembered you had asked my advice on fans who write to you about math anxiety.

This is my advice for anyone who feels an oncoming attack of math anxiety:

1) Stop what you are doing immediately, and sit down.
2) Close your eyes and take a deep, relaxing breath.
3) Then, slowly count to 10 using the number 2 in a base-4 numerical system

Also, always be on the lookout for trick math questions; they can only make you look stupid. Example: How many cookies in a biker's dozen? Answer: 3 at the very most, bikers *love* cookies. Or another example: What goes into thirteen twice? Answer: Roman Polanski (or Michael Jackson).

And finally, if numbers get to be too much, ignore them. It's a well known fact that Walt Disney hated watching 101 Dalmatians because he "always lost count." The same with Albert Einstein. He hated 101 Dalmatians too, but not for numerical reasons.

Until next time, Henry.

Rob Overton

6/29/93
Dear Henry,

Thank you for the information on where to find decorative tins for my mother's imported Danish butter cookies. I'm so glad to know there's someone out there in the world of rock and roll who loves Martha Stewart and her wonderful homemaking tips. Also, I read your article in <u>Quilting</u> magazine, and I think you have terrific ideas for alternate stitch patterns.

My 5-year old daughter Kelly loves both your children's records, but is especially fond of <u>NAP TIME</u> (she likes <u>FUN TIME</u> too). She really loves the songs "Frog Legs" and "Bull's Eye" and the song about the tattooed love boy. And she just goes crazy over the Henry Rollins punching bags they have at Toys-R-Us. She wants one for her birthday.

I understand the follow-up to <u>FUN TIME</u> is called <u>PLAY TIME</u> and will be out by Christmas. We can't wait.

I just wanted to say that I think what you are doing is wonderful, and I think that you are a perfect role model for these trying times. If the kids can see how far you have gone without the need for drugs or alcohol, then they truly have something to aspire to.

God Bless!

Karen Winokur
New Rochelle, NY

From the desk of... *Carol Caldecott*

Carol Caldecott
25450 Warner Ave.
Irvine, CA 92745 USA

7/1/93

Henry Rollins, I hope you're happy with yourself, corrupting the young, impressionable minds who listen to your children's records. My youngest son Timmy plays them over and over in an endless, mindless succession. I really wonder what possessed you to write a song called "Dead Animal Farm", or "Talk Back to Mommy", or "The Yelling Song" for that matter. And that idiotic song about boogers, how could you? I am certain that this is all a conscious effort on your part to corrupt our nation's youth. And I know that wherever you are, you are laughing at my expense.

And tell me this: Am I really supposed to get my son Billy a snake because Henry Rollins had snakes growing up? How can I tell him that it's just a phase he's going through, when it's clear-cut that you never grew out of that phase yourself?

And for God's sake think before you put so much focus on hate and death. Really, a book called <u>1000 Ways To Die</u>, or the new one, <u>Deathgrip</u>, couldn't possibly be beneficial for anyone to read. There are laws about the printing of this type of subject matter, and your name is on our list of undesirable writers and publishers.

Be warned.

Sincerely,

Carol Caldecott

Carol Caldecott

7/3/93
Henry—

I don't know what the hell I was thinking with that last letter.
Don't get me wrong, I think punctuation is important. But I
don't *just* want your Black Flag book to be grammatically
correct, I want it to be *more* than the sum of each of the
individual members of Black Flag. I want the book to add up,
so it's important that this sum we're talking about be the right
sum, okay? And more importantly, and help me out here,
because it's 4 in the morning and I'm riding a huge caffeine
wave that may never break, I want your book to be punctuated
with laughter. I want it to be so fucking funny that people pop
stitches, and not just stitches in their sides, I mean stitches in
their foreheads too. I want the Black Flag book to be so weird
that people have to think about why they're laughing, and
that's when they'll pop the stitches in their forehead. And I'm
not talking about Black Flag jokes, (i.e. how many members of
Black Flag does it take to stink up the van?), because we
promised Greg Ginn we'd stop razzing him in print (that's what
the restraining order from SST stated, right?).

Also, tell Tony the Frog to get off my back, okay? I'm sick of
his goddamn messages.

Butch the Oreo King

Dear Henry,

        I saw you on The Gil Evans Fishing Hour and was won-
dering how long it really takes before anyone starts catching
fish on that show. Is Gil Evans such a good fisherman that he
starts catching them right away? I guess he knows where to
look, but I think his use of a fish finder is cheating. (Did
you get a good look at his equipment? Did he use Interphase
Matrix Scanning Sonar? Were you using your own fishing gear?
It looked like you were using a Zebco Hypercast spinning reel
on some type of Fenwick graphite rod.)
        I could tell Gil was pissed that you caught three fish
before he even had a nibble, and I'm glad you got on his case
for moving his fishing line over to your side of the boat.
What a loser. Also, his snide remark about your spoken word
shows was out of line. So was the lame "die casting" joke he
made at your expense. I guess I shouldn't be surprised that he
was baiting you, after all, as a professional fisherman, it's
what he does for a living.
        I've watched the tape a bunch of times, even in slow
motion, and I still think your lure would have hooked Gil's
ear whether or not you had released on the reel's thumb-bar
sooner. Plus, if you replay the tape, you can see that Gil
craned his neck in your direction just as you were following
through on your cast, so it was his fault, not yours. I still
can't tell whether you pushed Gil out of the boat, or if he
just fell, but either way, it was classic. So was your reeling
him back to the boat by his ear. Jesus, did he look pissed.
        I liked that close up of your Panther Martin fishing
lure hanging from his ear. I can still hear your voice, Henry:
"Who's the punk now, Gil?" That was great.

        If you're ever on that show again, ask him if he likes
fish, and when he says yeah, flip him the bird and say "here's
a perch!"

Jeff Peterson   *Jeff Peterson*
Iowa City, IA

7/17/93

Dear Henry,

Let's sum up the situation. We've been playing Battle-
ship by mail for just over 5 months. So far, out of ten
moves, including the move you sent today, you haven't
had <u>any</u> misses. And I haven't had any hits. Don't you
find that a little odd? Perhaps one-sided?

I know you're corresponding with my sister, so you can
tell her that I've removed my Battleship board from my
room, and she's just going to have to guess the coordi-
nates from now on. I'm on to you Rollins. Your inside
job is over. Loose lips sink ships, and I'm talking
about your ships, Henry. This cheating of yours, even
though I can't prove it, will come back at you tenfold.

Your last call of A-9 sank my submarine, and you're
still batting one thousand. But I've still got 2 ships
left, and Lady Luck is sending a slump your way that
would make even Lou Gehrig slit his wrists.

My next call: D-8.

Start praying, Rollins.

SBP
Steve "Battleship" Potempkin
Austin, TX

LOCKHART & ASSOCIATES

NEW YORK · LOS ANGELES · BARSTOW

7/20/93

Henry,

As your publicist, I must inform you that Disney has threatened legal action on your most recent children's single, "Serendipity Doo Da", and it's references to Walt Disney's cryogenic state of "frozen animation." I suggest you change the lyrics. Perhaps the line "Walt's on the rocks" could be changed to "Waltz on the rocks," as it's the printed lyric that makes this a libel action. My feeling on this children's market is that although we've just tapped into a gold mine, there are certain concessions you must make.

Some good news: the <u>Where's Henry?</u> children's book that 2.13.61 has just made available to Europe and Australia is doing gangbusters business overseas. Don't worry about the recent litigation from the "Where's Waldo" people, I don't think they have a case. If they do take us to court we'll just have to rip them a new zip code like we did with that asshole from the Children's Television Workshop.

Also, a Japanese animation company has expressed interest in creating a Henry Rollins Saturday morning cartoon series, complete with little "smurf-like" Rollins characters with little blue tattoos. They've already had a few hit series (they did Speed Racer in the 60's). There might even be a breakfast cereal tie-in, or even better, an action figure toy.

I informed them that as your publicist, fielding offers is not one of my responsibilities, and I gave them your manager's number. You should be hearing from him soon.

Sincerely,

Larry Lockhart
Lockhart and Associates

400 N. SCHUSTER WAY STE. 900, BEVERLY HILLS, CA 90210 U.S.A.

Dear   Henry

Do   you   have   a
dog?   We   got   a
new   dog
his   name   is
Rambo.   You   can
see   him   if   you
come   to   my
birthday   party.

Your   friend   timey

Dear Smokey,  Smile

Ever since your show here in Raleigh, I haven't been able to sleep. If my parents knew you let me kiss you, they'd have a shit fit. It really sucks though because now you're gone, and you're all I can think about.

Do you make out with girls in every town? Jill's brother was teasing us, saying we're hopeless Rollins groupies. He says that first you're a fan, then you're a groupie who shows up at local gigs, then you're a groupie who travels all over to see the band on every date, like Deadheads. Then, eventually, because you're a familiar face, you start working for the band, running errands or even being a roadie and helping them set up every night, or, because you're dating the lead singer and he notices you have a good voice, you become a back-up singer and then you're part of the band. My brother said you were a Black Flag groupie in 1982, and then they asked you to join the band. Is that true? I never saw Black Flag. I was only two in 1982.

So is all this stuff about groupies for real? What about groupies that you get sick of? Plus, I never see any female roadies. In this thing on groupies on MTV, roadies from different bands said it was their job to pick out the cutest groupies and bring them backstage to meet the band. Is that how you met me? Jill said that sometimes people have to sleep with roadies just to get to meet the band. Did you ever sleep with the roadies?

Please write back to me, I want to know what you're thinking.

Love,

Kimberly Evans

Kimberly Evans
Raleigh, N.C.

8/1/93

Dear Henry,

What gives? First you get a hit with D-5, then before
you even sink the boat, you turn around and your next
call is another hit at completely different coordi-
nates. I can't figure you out, but I'd guess that
you've been reading The Art of War.

And then there's the matter of my misses. Are you
moving your ships, Henry, or just stacking them? This
isn't 3-Dimensional Battleship we're playing here, so
stacking is out of the question.

Anyway, you just got *another* hit. But what exactly
have you hit upon, Henry? Is it my Aircraft Carrier? Or
my Destroyer? Do you even care? Do you play by anyone's
rules?

Or is the key to this game something I have hit upon?
Some dark little secret of yours. I know that cheating
is what floats your boat, and now I see how all that
time on MTV guest vee-jaying with Kennedy has gone
right to your head. Or your neck.

And frankly, I've about had it with you, Henry. But
remember this: when your ship comes in, it will be
burned beyond recognition, and you will have to fight
tooth in hand just to get a leg up.

So the race is on.

Next move: E-8

SBP

Steve "Battleship" Potempkin
Austin, TX

8/3/93

Dear Henry,

Some words of advice on your current tour itinerary: *space* yourself. I know you've been going strong for ten years now and believe full well that a body in motion tends to stay in motion, but I must point out that in their studies of the law of inertia, physicists have neglected to take into account one very important factor: motion sickness. Everybody gets it, eventually.

Just know that when the music stops, there's always a chair to sit in. I know this concept of non-competitive musical chairs may seem radical — believe me, it is. You might even think it's boring, that it changes the focus of the game from survival (Will I get a chair?) to a more social realm (If I'm guaranteed a chair when the music stops, then who do I want to sit next to?). That may be true.

But know that there is a profound shift now occurring in our understanding of the nature of reality. Some call it a second Copernican revolution, the first Copernican revolution being the shift from the belief in Ptolemy's geocentric universe to the Copernican belief in a heliocentric one. The second Copernican shift combines the two by including inner space as well.

Your detractors may feel that "you think the world revolves around you" (geocentric), but at the same time you give your fans something to focus on (or around — heliocentric). So it's all relative. But there are extremes in each case: The egomaniac (geocentric) and the co-dependent with no sense of self (heliocentric). The shift now occurring involves striking a balance between both belief systems — a healthy ego that is non-threatening.

The good news, Henry, is that you don't have to do anything. Maybe just stop and snip the flowers a little more often.

Who knows, maybe the Second time around, they'll just give Jesus a rose. It beats nailing him up, right? No one dies and we all stand around laughing like it's the end of an episode of the Flintstones.

Rob Overton

Don't you think you're spreading yourself a little thin
these days Rollins? I can't turn on the TV or pick up
a magazine without your stupid face glaring back at me.
And what is this shit about children's records? All it
is, is "Rollins this" and "Rollins that." Jesus, if I
had a gun for every time some idiot rants about how
great you are. Read <u>The ANarchist's Cookbook,</u> or Abby
Hoffman's <u>SteaL This Book</u>. Now those are books you
should have on your press instead of all that angst
ridden drivel you crank out. Wake up and smell your
coffee, Rollins. You're a poser, and I'm on to you.
You're just the new flavor of the month and you're
boring me. You get X̶X̶X̶X̶X̶ 33 flavors to choose from, and
you pick vannilla.

But if there's one thing I am certain about these
days, it's that this world can do without HEnry
Rollins. How does that make you feel, Henry? DOes it
scare you? Well too bad. I think that this time <u>you</u>
have it coming. Ultimateley, it will all be your own
undoing anyway.

See you SOON,

CARL

PROJECT 213
P. O . BOX 2417
LOS ANGELES, CA 90036

8/11/93
Dear Henry,

I represent a young group of UFO abductees who are into the Rollins Band. We call ourselves Project 213. Think of us as a slight variation on Wharf Rats, the 12-step group of recovering Deadheads who have found that life after drugs and alcohol hasn't hampered their love and enjoyment of the Grateful Dead. There are over 400 members from all over the world in Project 213, and although we are just now coming to the fore, we have been together for more than 2 years. In a sense, it is your music that grounds us in the third dimension, enabling us to expose the Alien Conspiracy and World Government Cover-up of UFO Close Encounters.

I send you this letter primarily to let you know that we exist and are helping other Rollins fans know that they are not alone in their dealings with the growing alien tide. One fact that seems to consistently be buried in all of the available UFO literature is that teenagers and young adults—the core of your fan base—are prime targets for recruitment by the Zeta Reticula race commonly known as the Greys. I use the term "recruitment" in all earnestness, for although there are many abductees who are taken aboard the motherships against their will, our studies show that the bulk of teenagers are rarely abducted, but instead are *invited* onto the ships after being sold an army bill of goods on adventure that caters to the average teenager's overall dissatisfaction with life and growing alienation in this world, targeting the normal rebellious attitude that defines the life-phase of being a teenager or young adult.

A typical night out with the Greys would start with the aliens showing the teenagers how to work the controls of the mothership, letting the kids believe they are piloting the craft to whatever destination the Greys have chosen, thereby appealing to the teenager's reckless need for speed and abandon. Usually the ships end up in New Mexico, often toying with military radar screens and local air space, and engaging in occasional hi-tech space chase encounters with Air Force fighter jets. Many of these teenage "abductions" have shown a penchant for some "harmless" cow-tipping — an act that inevitably leads to some form of cattle mutilation. Also a favorite among teen abductees is the desecration of farmer's fields via the notorious "space graffiti" of crop circles that have been popping up in England and other parts of the world with growing regularity.

Please if possible include some information about Project 213 in your next newsletter. Thank you for your time, and remember: We are all protected by the Ashtar Command, the benevolent 5th dimensional race aiding us in our fight to reclaim Planet Earth.

Thank you,

Duane Andrews

Duane Andrews

UNDERWOOD MANAGEMENT • 3005 EREWHON PLACE • HOLLYWOOD, CA • 90036 • (310)777-POSE • FAX (310)777-2345

HEY HENRY—

I ASSUME THAT LOCKHART HAS ALREADY TOLD YOU ABOUT THE JAPANESE ANIMATION OFFERS. I KNOW HE CLAIMS THEY ACCIDENTALLY CALLED HIM, THINKING HE WAS "FIELDING OFFERS" FOR YOU, BUT I THINK HE'S TRYING TO MUSCLE IN ON SOME OF THE DEALS COMING YOUR WAY. YOU KNOW THE OLD ADAGE: NEVER TRUST A PUBLICIST. SO KEEP AN EYE ON HIM. HE'S TOO SMOOTH FOR HIS OWN GOOD.

ALSO, SEVERAL VIDEO GAME MANUFACTURERS HAVE APPROACHED ME ABOUT THE POSSIBILITY OF AN INTERACTIVE VIDEO GAME ABOUT THE ROLLINS BAND.

HERE ARE A FEW OF THE PROPOSED STORYLINES:

- A KID ARRIVES AT A ROLLINS SHOW, HAS PROBLEMS WITH THE GUY AT THE DOOR, WHO CLAIMS HE NEEDS AN I.D.

- THE ROAD CREW HAS PROBLEMS GETTING THE EQUIPMENT TO A GIG.

- WHERE'S HENRY? THE SHOW STARTS IN 15 MINUTES.

- ONSTAGE, HENRY CONTINUOUSLY KICKBOXES A MENACING GROUP OF NAZI SKINHEADS OUT TO GET HIM.

- THE BAND HAS PROBLEMS WITH A CLUB OWNER WHO REFUSES TO PAY.

- THERE'S A WEIRD GROUPIE WHO WON'T LEAVE HENRY ALONE.

- THE EQUIPMENT VAN IS STOLEN.

- HENRY GOES HOME WITH A WOMAN FROM THE SHOW, ONLY TO FIND OUT HER PARENTS ARE BOTH COPS.

THE GAME WOULD BE CALLED "SEARCH AND DESTROY", AND YOU WIN BY GETTING THE VAN TO THE NEXT GIG WITH ALL THE EQUIPMENT AND THE BAND MEMBERS INTACT.

AND HENRY, ABOUT THAT MANSON CONNECTION. USE IT! I SEE A FILM PROJECT: MANSON FAMILY ROBINSON. MAINLINE FILMS HAS SHOWN SOME INTEREST.

FINALLY, A GROUP SELLING 1994 MAYAN CALENDARS IS INTERESTED IN USING YOU AS A PINUP FOR ONE OF THEIR UPCOMING MONTHS.

GET BACK TO ME ON THIS AS SOON AS POSSIBLE.

SINCERELY,

KEITH UNDERWOOD
UNDERWOOD MANAGEMENT

8/27/93

Dear He~~~~

my next move, I'm just going
us winning streak of yours. Do
Henry? Or are you straight in
ing, no booze, no drugs. It
a just get "punch" drunk.

n going to stall. Why should
y Destroyer, you'd just rub it
ith the last three ships. But
Say what you have to say and
e. No one ever said anything
sportsmanship award.

er yet. You may have downed
t was a thermos of that cheap
know and I know that even
will eventually crash and
ke, baby, but don't come
you in the ass.

ed)

SBP

Steve "Battleship" Potempkin
Austin, TX

9/1/93

Dear Henry,

      Our high school English teacher, Mr. Butts, said we
could do a book report on anything we wanted, and I chose
<u>Pissing in the Gene Pool</u>. Then when he found out I was doing
your book, he tried to limit my selection to those books in
the school library. He finally agreed, but said if I was so
bent on doing a report on your book, maybe I could ask you
some questions about your "first hand writing experience."
He's trying to make me look stupid for choosing your book, but
he's also slamming you, thinking you won't help me.

      So my question for you about the book is whether or
not you feel the narrator is trustworthy. Are you the narra-
tor? Or is it a persona that goes out on tour and writes the
books? And if the narrator isn't trustworthy, why is the book
worth reading? How do I know you're telling the truth?

      Mr. Butts thinks reading literature is about finding
the truth. And everybody knows that truth is stranger than
fiction. But if truth is stranger than fiction, why would
anyone read fiction? For me, the weirder the better. So
fiction is just changing the names and places so none of your
friends know you're writing about them. And I guess something
in the process gets lost. My mom reads Anne Tyler, and those
books are so boring, they must be fiction.

      If you could just tell me what was going on in your
mind when you wrote <u>Pissing in the Gene Pool</u>, that would be
great. I know the book is all about your thoughts, but what
were you thinking when you wrote them? The thoughts behind the
thoughts. Also, would you say that "Man's Inhumanity Towards
Man" is a theme that runs through <u>Pissing In the Gene Pool</u>?
What about "Man Vs. Nature" or "Man Vs. Himself"? Any other
themes you can think of would be helpful. And any information
on the book's structure.

      Your newsletter says you're in Europe, so I hope you
get this by the time my book report is due next month.

See ya,

Jeff Peterson
Iowa City, IA

9/3/93

Dear Henry,

In checking into your publicist's background, as requested, I discovered some curious bits of information. Before Lockhart worked for Geffen (where, incidentally, he was fired — a fact he lied to you about), he was in the marketing division at Toyco, a large toy manufacturing company, where he was also fired, supposedly after heading an ill-fated marketing campaign for the Buddy Ebsen doll and bringing the company to its knees, financially. So you might want to keep an eye on this publicist of yours, especially when he starts pitching marketing strategies for anything Rollins-related.

Also, I talked to the Mayan Calendar people, and there seems to be a delay at their end regarding the look of the calendar itself. Apparently, the shift into a fourth dimensional time frame has not been as easy as expected, and in the change to the 13 moon solar year, certain problems have arisen. First, the Mayan Calendar Commission has yet to reach an agreement on the proposed name for the 13th month that this system calls for. And more problematically, the exact placement of the additional month enters into the equation as well. It's not as simple as just putting this new month between March and April, or as their marketing executive suggested, "somewhere toward the end of the year, when all the months seem to blend together anyway."

The final snag in their plans is that the Mayan Calendar format is not as precise as they had hoped it would be. With 13 months each based on a 28 day lunar cycle, there is at the end of every calendar year, one day left over (13 months x 28 days = 364 days). On the current 12 month calendar, there is an extra day every four years. But with one extra day per year, they're not sure whether they should shift the "bonus" day to the end of a different month every year, or stick with the current system and put it at the end of February. With the latter arrangement, not only is every month a February (with 28 days), but with February having 29 days, every year is a non-confusing leap year.

And all this trouble just to add more pin-up photos? Why not shift to a 12 month calendar where each month consists of three 10-day metric weeks, where you could have 3 pin-ups per month as opposed to just one?

I'll talk to you soon.

Rob Overton

Dear Henry,

Due to a miraculous set of unusual events, I have been cured of my recent affliction at the Juvenile Detention Center Infirmary in my home town. But unfortunately, because I regained my health, the director of the Detention Center, who is really a dick, decided to make an example of me and send me to the State Prison here in Waupun, Wisconsin. Unless my attorney can pull some strings and get me out of the Big House, I will be here for the rest of my life (they are very strict here in Wisconsin about aggravated assault and grand theft auto).

So, needless to say, I have a little time on my hands and would really appreciate a response to this letter. I will forgive you for still not sending any letters, even when I was on my deathbed. But now that I'm in prison, I expect a response. I don't want to make this sound like a threat, but who knows what kind of connections I might make here on the inside — connections with dangerous people who will be getting out soon and would be glad to get in touch with you.

My situation is the same as when I was in the Juvenile Detention Center. Since they don't let me receive mail here at the prison, I have to rely on my mother smuggling mail to me here in my barren cell once a month when she has visitation rights. So you can send letters to me "care of" my mom (Betsy) at my house in Janesville, WI.

Please hurry. I don't know how long I can last here. There are rats and the food is horrible, and everyone is mean to me because I'm the new guy. To pass time, I play the harmonica and bang my tin cup on the bars of my cell. Plus the warden and the guards are always threatening me with solitary confinement.

I hope to hear from you soon.

Sincerely,
Rusty Jenkins

Rusty J.

9/16/93

Miss, oh excuse me, Miss!

Miss, you dropped your bomb, but it didn't hit any
ships. Oh Miss!

You hit water this time, Rollins. How does it feel? Do
you feel small? Well, I'm not going to rub it in your
face too much. In fact, I will be a true gentleman and
give you my next move: I-5.

Touché.

SBP

Steve "Battleship" Potempkin
Austin, TX

Dear Henry,

Who'da thought that the Nuge would have his own book in the Rock Bible. These truly are the end times. I know there's a chapter on urban assault vehicles and three-wheeling, but I wondered what the hell Ted does up in Detroit during the winter. In the BOOK OF TED, does he talk about snowmobiling? I also heard that he was breeding hybrid "Super-Llamas", a genetically superior llama that can spit twice as far as any Portuguese longshoreman, even on a windy day.

Have you heard from Butch "the Oreo King" lately? He keeps sending my brother these weird letters about sod-busting. What he does is, he finds out where houses are getting new lawns, then the night after the sod is put down, they roll it back up and load it onto a truck. Usually they only do half lawns, due to time constraints (they have to meet the sod-quota). He says it's a lot like toilet-papering.

Butch told me that he had been to a psychic — a child psychic, who was only 10 years old. Instead of a Tarot deck, the kid used baseball cards. Butch was really freaked, because the first card that was turned over was a Roberto Clemente Commemorative. Then the kid told him to "have as much fun in the next 3 weeks as possible."

Are you going to be out in Jersey at all this winter? At your last show in Trenton, the owner of the club made an announcement about "No square dancing!" Did he mean slam dancing? I think you'd be great as a caller for square dancing Rollins fans. "Allemande Left," or "Promenade!" — those words would just roll off your tongue, Henry, and you'd have that crowd in the palm of your hand (Not that you don't already!).

I have to get going, but I'm going to be in L.A. from February 12th to the 18th, so I hope we can meet up for a second.

Take it easy, Henry.

Lyle

Your pal Lyle Wilcox

P.S. Remember: You don't have to get drunk to play the Whiskey.

Federal Bureau of Investigation
Washington D.C.   20007

9/25/93
Dear Mr. Rollins,

Our New Jersey Office was recently notified by local authorities of a
Trenton man named Carl Plaske under suspicion of U.S. Mail fraud.
Further investigation has led us to believe that this man is mentally
unstable and may pose a personal threat to you. It is because of your
celebrity notoriety and this case's interstate status that our Bureau is now
involved.

On September 19, 1993, our office obtained a search warrant and entered
the apartment of Carl Plaske. Strewn across the room were several of your
books and tapes. A trail of artificial blood led to a closet, in which we
came across what can only be described as a "hate altar". There were
magazine clippings and other items pertaining to you pinned to a bulletin
board. Among these items: a complete 1993 tour itinerary for the Rollins
Band, including European and American dates; and pictures of you with
your head circled in red magic marker as well as pictures with your head
ripped off and pinned over to the side. Hate slogans and death threats
directed at you filled the entire bulletin board.

The current whereabouts of Carl Plaske are unknown, and we have federal
warrants for his arrest in 31 states. Please notify us if this man attempts to
make contact with you. We have enclosed a picture of Plaske for your use
in making a positive identification.

An agent from our Los Angeles Bureau will be in further contact with you.

Sincerely,

Special Agent Roger Goodman
Federal Bureau of Investigation
New Jersey Branch

Dear Smokey,

My parents are really mad because I got a tattoo. It's a small one on my ankle of a snake. They grounded me and went through my things. My mom read my diaries and got all wigged about what she thinks is my obsession with you. Then my dad got all mad because my mom read him the part about how I kissed you at your last show here in town.

So don't come to town, Smokey. My dad's pissed and he might confront you. He has a real temper.

I'm not supposed to write to you anymore, but I don't care.

Love,

Kimberly Evans

Kimberly Evans
Raleigh, N.C.

10/5/93

Dear Henry,

I can't believe you'd stoop so low as to accuse me of
moving my own ships, even though I'm beginning to
wonder if you even have any ships on your own board.
What was it about that last miss of yours that bothered
you so much, Henry? Do you know something I don't know?
Have you been talking to my sister again? I think you
have, because you just got another hit.

So quit whining about my board setup and focus on your
own ghost ships.

Next move: J-6

SBP

Steve "Battleship" Potempkin
Austin, TX

Dear Henry,

Thanks for your tips on <u>Pissing in the Gene Pool</u>.
I have another book-related question for you. I'm
reading a used copy of Joseph Conrad's <u>Heart of Darkness</u> for
class and whoever had it before me highlighted it with a blue
highlighter. Is there such a thing in English Lit as an
untrustworthy reader? Should I trust whoever read it before me
and just read the blue parts?

The other thing is that he stopped reading in the
middle of chapter three, because the highlighter ends there.
Or maybe he didn't stop reading there, but he did stop high-
lighting, and that means that the rest of the book is worth
reading. But if he did stop reading at chapter three, then
it's probably not worth reading, right? Have you read <u>Heart of
Darkness</u>? Is it any good? Our teacher said the movie <u>Apoca-
lypse Now</u> was based on it, and I know from the interview in
that skateboarding magazine that it's your favorite movie.
It's mine too, along with <u>Terminator 2</u>.

Also, this girl Mary Clare said you can get brain
seizures from smoking clove cigarettes. She heard about it in
Germany. Is that true? You've been to Germany. Is it only true
for German clove cigarettes?

See ya,

Jeff Peterson
Iowa City, IA

ROLLINS—
YOU SUCK.
HOW MUCH OF YOUR
MAIL IS HATE MAIL?
ONLY HALF?
MAYBE I CAN RAISE
THE PERCENTAGE.
YOUR DEAD.
—CARL

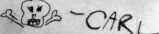

LA MUNICIPALIDAD DE LOS
ANGELES — ALCALDIA
M-071   LOS ANGELES CITY HALL

POST CARD

ROLLINS—
P.O. BOX 1910
LA CA 90078

AN OFFICIAL
PRODUCT

POST CARD

2.13.61 MAILROOM

Gary— Forward to H.R. or
to Agent Goodman?

10/19/93
Dear Henry,

I can now verify, without a doubt, that Larry Lockhart is the man solely responsible for selling Toyco on the marketability of the Buddy Ebsen doll and getting the project green-lighted. After that, his role is a bit hazy. What follows is a case history of Toyco's Buddy Ebsen doll, a case in which Lockhart's "business savvy" results in more than just a mere textbook example of miscalculated audience appeal.

First off, I will say this about the situation, Henry. Either Lockhart's a brilliant salesman, or the people at Toyco are incredibly stupid and Lockhart's a con man. When the Buddy Ebsen dolls hit the toy store shelves in 1987, Toyco was marketing a doll based on an actor whose most recent television series had been off prime time television for 7 years, but had maintained popularity through syndication on the two "nostalgia" channels — A&E and Nickelodeon.

To Lockhart and the marketing division at Toyco, the success of the Buddy Ebsen doll hinged entirely on one key question: Would the Buddy Ebsen doll have the crossover appeal that Kenner's Joe Mannix doll had in the late 60's? Curiously, the answer is both yes and no. Joe Mannix was a character played by actor Mike Connors. Buddy Ebsen is an actor who has enjoyed success on not one, but two top-rated prime-time television shows in a time span of 20 years. This was complicated by the fact that the Buddy Ebsen doll was a gender-neutral doll targeted at both boys and girls, as opposed to a gender specific doll like Hasbro's G.I. Joe. One could easily forget that the reason the Joe Mannix doll had crossover appeal was that the set included his secretary Peggy and her desk.

At first glance, the advance orders and initial brisk sales of the Buddy Ebsen doll would indicate that the marketing plan was in fact reaching Lockhart's desired target audience of boys and girls between the ages of 4 and 10. However, as the return/exchange rate on the dolls soon surpassed sales, it became obvious that something had gone awry.

Toyco's earliest assessment of the problem was that these astute young viewers were confused about the doll. Were they getting Jed Clampett or Barnaby Jones? Further research revealed the unfortunate truth: children were simply bored with the Buddy Ebsen doll. The doll lacked what other detective dolls in the past had made up for. The Starsky and Hutch and Knightrider action sets both came with cars, and the popular Miami Vice action figures were equipped with drug-running planes and real firearms. The Buddy Ebsen doll had glaucoma and a heart problem.

Toyco viewed their problem as twofold: 1) Their target audience of children normally interested in dolls was not interested in Buddy Ebsen. 2) The people who are interested in Buddy Ebsen, namely the 25 million weekly viewers of The Beverly Hillbillies and Barnaby Jones, are much too old to be interested in dolls.

But Toyco's conclusion that the fans of Buddy Ebsen were too old to be interested in dolls was not entirely accurate. In-store surveys at Toys-R-Us revealed that a large number of people between the ages of 25 and 40 had purchased the Buddy Ebsen dolls as gag gifts for friends. Thus, it was obvious that, to the baby-boomers, Buddy Ebsen had camp appeal.

But to the 100,000 members of the Official Buddy Ebsen Fan Club, "camp appeal" meant that the doll was not being bought "in the true spirit of a Buddy Ebsen fan." So, after receiving stacks upon stacks of letters and petitions from irate Buddy Ebsen Fan Club members (including Richard Nixon and Lockhart's own father, Walter), Toyco decided to recall an unprecedented 50,000 dolls—the largest of its kind since Mattel's recall of Barbie spin-off Malibu Floozy in 1975, due to parental pressure.

One thing is certain, in the toy industry, sales are sales. Lockhart's Buddy Ebsen doll had found an audience — it just wasn't his intended audience. Had Toyco not decided to cave into the fear of public disapproval, they might have recouped their initial losses. Whether the toy is purchased for a child or an adult is beside the point, really, but I certainly wouldn't give Lockhart much credit for his dumb luck. And I don't know how far I would trust him as your publicist in dealing with this public he seems to have no feel for. Let's get real, Henry. The issue here is that Lockhart was able to sell the idea of a Buddy Ebsen doll. A Buddy Ebsen Doll! I could see Buddy Ebsen pushing Depends or maybe colostomy bags ("Brown Bag it for life with Buddy Ebsen Colostomy Bags"), but a Buddy Ebsen doll?

Lockhart is dangerous, Henry. Proceed with caution in your future dealings with this man. Parental discretion is advised.

Rob Overton

Carol Caldecott
25450 Warner Ave.
Irvine, CA 92745 USA

From the desk of... *Carol Caldecott*

10/27/93

Dear Mr. Rollins,

Do you think it's a coincidence that you arrive in L.A for a three day period and in that three day period the entire town catches fire? Some people have highly combustible personalities, but you Henry Rollins have the ability to burn down entire regions of Southern California. So cut it out. Everyone knows that you and your music are responsible for the outbreak of the L.A. riots. It's right there in the court transcripts.

And one more string of coincidences: your appearances on both the Dennis Miller show and the Chevy Chase show. Both of these talk shows were canceled. Don't you think that's a little strange? The Tonight Show hasn't been canceled. David Letterman hasn't been canceled. But then, you haven't been on those shows.

So here is a suggestion: Do everyone a favor and use the reverse-Midas touch that you have on talk shows to our advantage. Go on Geraldo. And Donahue. They are both horrible men. They are not Christian, and they are both responsible for the smut that my son Timmy and other children are seeing on television when they come home from school.

You may wonder how I know you are in town for three days, but as I've told you before, we are watching you Mr. Rollins, and have been for some time. So straighten up and fly right.

This is your last warning.

Sincerely,

Carol Caldecott

Carol Caldecott

11/1/93

Seasons Greetings to all Tee-Totalers out in the Bunker!!

With winter coming on, it is easier than you think to keep your golf swing in shape until next spring. So don't waste your money on orange balls for snow golf, when you can set up shop right in the privacy of your own home.

It's simple, especially if your living room has plush, wall-to-wall carpeting. If it doesn't, go to the local Carpetland in the guise of a prospective buyer (Know dimensions of the room to appear legit — talk square footage.). Bring home several samples and tape them to your wood or linoleum floors. These carpet samples will provide a grass-like surface on which to practice your swing, while simultaneously protecting the floor from linoleum gouges or wood scrapes.

The first step is to clear all the furniture away from the middle of the room, because you'll need as much space to work with as possible. Open the sliding glass doors leading to the backyard according to your golf handicap (If you don't have sliding glass doors, get them.). As a general rule, the farther you are from the glass doors, the wider you will want them opened (Ken Green stands 10 feet from his glass doors and has them opened 2 1/2 feet. But then again, he's a professional.).

A good formula to use would be the basic slope and y-intercept equation, $y = mx + b$, with x being the distance you are from the glass doors, and y being how far the doors should be open. The variable m is a constant relative to your golf dexterity quotient, and b is your overall confidence ratio, having to do with alertness, pent up anxiety, and general cockiness.

After you've figured your distances, get a 3-wood from your Dad's sports closet and a ball from your shag bag. Use real balls, and not the wiffle-type golf balls, as they tend to throw you off when you get back to playing real golf courses in the spring. Make sure that there is at least 20 feet of headway after the ball has cleared the sliding glass doors. Of course, an open field would be ideal, but if you don't have that 20 foot clearance, the brick wall or aluminum siding of the building right next to yours will suffice.

Following your practice, cover any carpet divots with a magazine rack or one of your mother's plants. In fact, it's probably best to tee-off on a section of the floor that is normally covered by a larger piece of furniture, like a Lazyboy. The last thing you want to tee-off is your mom.

NOTE: If you live in a basement apartment, you can still practice this driving method. Pretend that one wall is where the sliding glass doors would be if you had them, and place masking tape on this wall to designate the distance that the two doors would be opened. Stand at least 15 feet away from the wall, and let it rip. As an added safety precaution, you might want to wear hockey pads and a helmet. (Anybody who's ever been winged by a Top-Flite while shagging balls at the local driving range will understand why).

KEEP IN THE SWING OF THINGS!

Your golf guru,
Chip Taylor

11/10/93

Dear Henry,

   I'm in detention because Mr. Butts, my tightass En-
glish teacher, claims I said "fuck" intentionally when it was
my turn to read out loud in class. We were reading <u>The Adven-
tures of Huckleberry Finn</u>, and I accidentally said "Fuck"
instead of "Huck". It really was an accident, but he's had it
in for me ever since someone toilet-papered his house at
Halloween (they fooled him by doing it the night before). I
know who did it, but I'm not going to say anything.
   And my Dad is really pissed at me these days, too
(more pissed than when I told him I wasn't going out for
football), because last weekend when my parents were at a
football game, my friend Jay and I branded two of our cows (my
neighbor Bob makes branding irons, and I had him make one of
the Black Flag symbol — the 4 rectangles). My mom and dad were
really cheesed off. They grounded me permanently and told me I
couldn't play your CD's anymore or read your books.
   It wasn't like I could just go wash the brands off. I
wish that was the case, though. Before we decided on branding
the cows, our first idea was to shave some puppies and tattoo
them, but they wouldn't sit still long enough with the clip-
pers. We discussed the pros and cons and figured that if we
tattooed the puppies, we'd have to keep them shaved just to
see the tattoos. That'd be a drag, but the good thing would be
that shaved puppies don't shed. Or we could let the hair grow
back and the tattoos would be our secret, like that guy who
had the treasure map tattooed on the top of his head and then
grew his hair out.
   I'm not supposed to write to you anymore, but there's
a lot of time to do things when I'm at school.

See ya,

Jeff Peterson

Jeff Peterson
Iowa City, IA

LOCKHART & ASSOCIATES

NEW YORK · LOS ANGELES · BARSTOW

11/12/93

Henry,

How is your hand? My face is still puffed up, but the x-rays showed no concussion, and I'm not going to press charges.

As your ex-publicist, I wanted to say that it has been a pleasure being your publicist and I'm sorry we had to part under such less than satisfactory circumstances. I would guess that it hurt you as much to fire me as it hurt me to be fired.

I've never actually been fired before, so it's been quite a blow to my ego. (Contrary to the rumors about my departure from Geffen Records, my decision there to leave was mutually agreed to by all parties involved).

I know we disagreed on how I was handling your image, but I think I did an exceptional job at times in handling your press and public. The Gil Evans fishing boat debacle is a case in point. By agreeing to pay all medical costs for the removal of the fishing lure from his ear (including tetanus shots and minor plastic surgery), I was able to hush him up before he even considered going to the press. The same in my dealings with that angry Parent's Coalition.

In retrospect, however, I do agree with you that had I handled the incident at Puppet Town differently, it never would have been blown so far out of proportion in the press. The same with the Children's Television Workshop. At least you can't say that I never got you a TIME magazine cover.

If you should reconsider my services, please call.

Sincerely,

Larry Lockhart
Lockhart and Associates

Dear Henry,

I figure you don't want me to call you Smokey anymore. I'm sorry about everything that happened. If I hadn't gotten a tattoo on my ankle, my parents never would have gone through my diaries, and my dad wouldn't have gone down to your show to hassle you. I wasn't allowed to go to your show, but Jill was there. She said my dad was yelling at you from the side of the stage, and when you told him to shut up, he went ballistic. I know you have people run at you alot on stage, and since he was off duty there was no way you could have known my dad was a cop.

Are you mad that I didn't tell you my dad was a cop? I was afraid that if I told you, you wouldn't want anything to do with me or my letters. I know you've had problems with the police in the past, so I decided not to say anything.

I know my dad tried to raise a stink, and I'm glad that the night court judge saw things your way and asked my dad to drop his charges. Thanks for not suing us. It's not the first time he's gotten a black eye in a scrape like that.

Anyway, I'm sorry about everything, and I hope there are no hard feelings.

Sincerely,

Kimberly Evans

Kimberly Evans
Raleigh, N.C.

P.S. Merry Christmas

MᴄBᴀɪɴ Mɪʟɪᴛᴀʀʏ Aᴄᴀᴅᴇᴍʏ

114 Cᴀʟʟɪsᴛᴇʀ Rᴅ., Aɴɴᴀᴘᴏʟɪs, MD 21401

Joseph Plaske, Chief Executive Administrator

11/19/93

Dear Mr. Rollins,

Following my son Carl's arrest and subsequent institutionalization, he has repeatedly told me to "get Henry." And although these are the only words he ever speaks (aside from some early mumblings about "backstage elves on Santa's guest list"), I assume he wants me to get in contact with you. The institution where he is currently residing does not allow its patients to have writing instruments of any kind, so I have transcribed from his 12' x 12' rubber cell wall a letter he wrote with saliva and blood during the incident:

> Henry Henry we all scream for Henry
> Take his curly shoes and run from the cave

If you have any insight into what this may mean, please contact me at the address above.

Thank you. I am sorry if my son has caused you any personal anguish.

Sincerely,

Joseph Plaske

Dear Henry,

When you're on the Ӿroad and you're in a city where you're
pretty sure no one knows who you are — not L.A. or New YorK,
probably a medium-sized city like Las Vegas or Atlanta — and your
show's over and you have the rest of the night off and you can
take it easy because you don't leave for the next city on your
tour until tomorrow morning — when you have that time to kick
back, do you ever go down to the corner store and stock up on
Butterfingers and Baby Ruth bars and Starburst and Reese's Peanut
Butter Cups and Munch Bars and Fritos, only to find that just as
you're at the counter and the guy is ringing it all up, you decide
you want Tootsie P̶o̶p̶ Rolls and M&M's and some Mountain Dew and a
package of Fun Size Snicker Bars — hopefully on sale because it's
after Halloween? And there, at the counter you suddenly flash on
all this candy you've bought — more candy than you've had in a
year with your strict Vegetarian diet — and you become verry self-
conscious because you're holding up the line with your last minute
decision-making and you hear the people behind you getting impa-
tient, shifting their weight initially and then eventualy com-
plaining out loud, so you decide to put up the hood on your
sweatshirt to avoid any peripheral eye-contact with them and then
you start worrying that the guy behind the ̶c̶l̶e̶r̶kcounter might think
you are putting up your hood because you want to rob the place,
but before you know it you've made your purchase and are on the
street, walking briskly at first and then running flat out, hoping
to sneak back to your hotel room unnoticed, so you can lock the
door behind you and turn on the TV and just relax .
Safe inside your hotel room, you dim the lights and take
off your clothes and turn on the TV, stopping for some reason at
the Home Shopping NEtwork. You immddiately become transfixed and
within a few seconds are so lost in what you see for sale on the
screen that you neglect to notice you have systematically pulled
the wrappers off of all the candy you bought and have stacked each
of the candy bars and individual Fritos into a pyramid-shaped
mound at the end of your bed. And then, almost in the blink of an
eye, your candy and soda and chips have ̶a̶l̶l disappeared and you
have a bit of a stomach ache, but this doesn't matter because in
the sugar and caffeine high that is mounting, you find yourself
in a state of euphoria, on the phone with your credit card,
ordering earrings and patio furniture and make-up kits, and before
you know it you have maxed out your credit card and are rummaging
through your stuff — the QVC operator still on hold — to find the
information from your manager's credit card that he gave you in
case of an emergency. ̶B̶Ҳ̶I̶X̶I̶Һ̶Е̶Ҳ̶Ҳ̶Ӯ̶Ḅ̶Ҳ̶Ҳ̶Ḅ̶Ҳ̶Ḅ̶I̶Һ̶Е̶Ḅ̶V̶Е̶Ҏ̶Ҳ̶I̶Һ̶Ӓ̶I̶Ҳ̶Ҳ̶Ӯ̶Ḅ̶Ҳ̶Һ̶Ӓ̶V̶Е̶Ҳ̶Ҳ̶Ҳ
Thank God you find the information and you are able to get a
pretty set of matching lamps for next to your davenport and a car
-seat cover for those hot summer days, to name a few items. When
his card is maxed out you decide to stop for the evening, and as
you hang-up from that final purchase, you realize that all of the
stuff you purchased with your manager's credit card will be sent
to your manager's home address because in your sugar- induced
stupor, you couldnt think straight and were reading directly off
of the sheet of paper in frontof you, giving them his billing

address as the shipping address, instead of your own
address. mMad at first, youdecide to shrug it off, telling
yourself that when your manager finds out his credit card
was used, you'll be able to convince him that sometime while
he was on tour, someone fun-lifted his wallett and was able
to get it back to him before he even knew it was missing.
You pass out on the bed from sheer exhaustion, and wake up
with an incredible sugar hangover just before the phone
rings for your 7 AM Wake- up call, wondering if maybe this
time you will suffer from buyer's remorse.

        I feel this way all the time, Henry. And I know you
do too.

Lynn Weir

Dear Henry,

Thanks for <u>finally</u> sending a letter. I have some good news to tell you. The State Prison officials at Waupun have come to their senses and realized just how wrong it is for me, a young teenager, to be in prison and on death row. So they decided by a unanimous vote to let me go on good behavior. Of course, I'll have to meet with a parole officer once a week and the State requires that I live at home until I graduate from High School, but things are looking up. So you can send your next letter directly to me here at home in Janesville, Wisconsin.

I expect to hear from you soon!

Sincerely,
Rusty Jenkins

Rusty J.

12/3/93

Fight fire with fire I always say, Rollins, so don't
piss on my back and then tell me it's raining.

So you've had 4 misses in a row. So what? Maybe I _am_
moving my aircraft carrier. Or maybe it just mysteri-
ously moved to new coordinates and you're experiencing
a kind of Bermuda Triangle. If that is the case, Henry,
then this game is operating outside of space and time.
And it could go on forever.

But then maybe the game stops here. Maybe that last hit
of yours 5 moves ago sank my carrier. Just because it
has 5 holes doesn't mean it has to be hit 5 times, does
it? Maybe there was one isolated hit with no more hits
to be found in the immediate vicinity. And maybe then
my aircraft carrier limped away and slowly sank into
oblivion. Besides, you were winning this game anyway.
And that's all this really is to you, isn't it? A game.

So I hereby stop this game and declare myself the
winner.

And you Henry Rollins are a choking squirrel loser.

SBP

Steve Potempkin
Austin, TX

P.S. Stay off the Internet, the Information Super
Highway frowns on hitchhikers and lurkers like you.

Dear Henry,

   I can't wait until I'm old enough to do whatever I want. I hate how my parents try and control my every move. It helps to know that you don't think it was my fault for everything that happened, but I still feel stuck here. I guess I have no choice but to wait until I'm out of school, unless I decide to quit early.

   I'm wishing you a Happy Birthday early, because I don't think I'll be writing much any more.

Sincerely,

Kimberly Evans
Kimberly Evans
Raleigh, N.C.

Carol Caldecott
25450 Warner Ave.
Irvine, CA 92745 USA

From the desk of... **Carol Caldecott**

12/18/93

Dear Mr. Rollins,

Don't think for a second that I don't see what you're doing. It's subtle,
I'll give you that. Hiding behind this drug-and-alcohol-free image.
Everyone focuses on that aspect, and they neglect to hear your real
message.

And tell me, just because we picketed your show on Saturday, is that a
reason to dedicate that horrible song "Pigfucker" to me? It wasn't just
"dedicated to the picketers outside," it was "for Carol Caldecott and her
ignorant coalition imposing on your 1st Amendment rights." I also
thought that bit about born-again Christians having two bellybuttons
was uncalled for. I know what you said, I've heard the tape. We have
insiders too, you know. So don't think the restraining order you filed
against me Monday is going to stop us.

You, Henry Rollins, are setting an example for our children, and you
must maintain a consistent attitude toward cleaning up your act.

The end times are near, and Judgment Day is upon us. It is time that
you come down off your high horse and repent for your sins.

Sincerely,

Carol Caldecott

Carol Caldecott

12/19/93

Dear Henry,

I just read the letters that the Battleship nut in Austin sent you, and it's not so obvious what kind of game this guy wants to play. According to James P. Carse, there are really only two types of games: finite games and infinite games. Finite games are played for the purpose of winning, and infinite games are played for the sole purpose of continuing the play. All games can fall into both categories, and this Austin man seems to enjoy the playing as much as the winning, even though in this case (and probably most others) he's a loser.

Also, his interpretation of the time/space continuum, although meant as a threat, is laughable. He is correct in describing Battleship as 2-Dimensional (a game played on a flat surface), but the real problem with Steve Potempkin's understanding of the nature of reality is the common misconception that the first three dimensions have to do with spatial coordinates. It's not as simple as adding length and width to get 2-D, then adding height to get 3-D. In fact, each of the planes (or dimensions) is organized according to levels of density, and although the first three dimensions *do* combine to form our physical reality, it is actually for electromagnetic reasons combined with conscious thought.

Also, because physical reality is meant to be experienced within the context of a time frame, this dimension of time added to a "supposed" 2-Dimensional game would make it 3-Dimensional, and therefore by extension anything we do within the context of 3-Dimensional reality combined with time makes our reality 4th Dimensional.

I will say that he is correct about the possibility of operating outside of space and time, but it has more to do with being in the moment, in the "now" where you can tap into infinite interdimensional possibilities. And outside of this moment, there are parallel realities. There is a parallel reality where he won the game of Battleship, just as there is a parallel reality where you are the owner of the pet store you used to work at. So if all possible scenarios are happening simultaneously in an infinite number of parallel realities, why not make this reality the one where you kill Steve Potempkin?

Until next time, Henry.

Rob Overton

12/20/93

Henry—

These lyrics came to me in a dream I had about Woodstock II:

> I came upon a child of God
> She was walking along the road
> And I asked her "Where are you going?"
> And this she told me:
>
> She said, "I'm going down to Yasgur's Farm
> I'm going to join in a rock and roll band
> I'm going to camp out on the land..."

And then the phone rang. Anyway, I know you in the 2.13.61 offices have been thinking about this, so I'm going to come right out and say it.

Five words, Henry, just five words:

CROSBY, STILLS, NASH AND ROLLINS

It makes complete sense to me, but then again, so did most of the Manson murders. Everybody knows you don't fuck with Charlie, 'cause Charlie don't surf.

Butch the Oreo King

Dear Henry,
could you wriet
more songs about
boogers?
your friend
timmy

12/29/93

Dear Henry,

No one ever died from a game of Battleship, it's not
some teen psycho game like Dungeons and Dragons.

So what do you say, how about 2 out of 3?

SBP

Steve "Battleship" Potempkin
Austin, TX

I WANT TO THANK HENRY ROLLINS AND EVERYONE IN THE 2.13.61 OFFICES (GARY I., CHRIS, KIRK, MODI, AND KATO THE KONQUEROR), AS WELL AS STAN AND DAVE AT ENDLESS FOR ALL THEIR HELP IN GETTING THIS BOOK MADE.

SPECIAL THANKS TO GEORGE GARY, MARY CLARE LINGEL, GARY TIECHE, LARRY LINSEY ("THE TRAVELER"), AND ANDRE BURKE FOR THEIR INVALUABLE INPUT ALONG THE WAY; ALSO TO LUKE DELL'AMICO FOR HIS HELP (AND DUANE AND DEBORAH), AND PATTY CLARK. I ALSO WANT TO THANK MY MOM AND DAD FOR THEIR SUPPORT AND FOR RESCUING ME BACK FROM THAT BRIEF BUT ILL-FATED STINT IN THE CIRCUS.

IF YOU HAVE ANY QUESTIONS ABOUT THIS BOOK OR ANY OF THE OTHER BOOKS OFFERED BY 2.13.61 PUBLICATIONS, WRITE TO HENRY, BECAUSE HENRY NOT ONLY LOVES YOUR LETTERS, MORE IMPORTANTLY, HENRY LOVES YOU! ANY QUESTIONS ABOUT THE BOSTON BRUINS MAY BE DIRECTED TO CHRIS MILLER C/O 2.13.61, AND FINALLY, ANY GENERAL QUESTIONS ABOUT NEW ZEALAND CAN BE ANSWERED BY KIRK GEE (SPECIFIC INQUIRIES RE: THE AVERAGE WINTER RAINFALL OUTSIDE OF AUCKLAND COMPARED TO, SAY, WELLINGTON ARE WELCOME, BUT PLEASE, NO QUESTIONS ABOUT THE GLOW WORMS OF MILFORD SOUND).